FREDDY'S EVEREST DIARY
THE DREAM OF FREDERICK T. BEAR

PAT FALVEY is a motivational speaker, adventurer and expedition leader. He has completed over 38 expeditions and is the only Irish person to have completed the Seven Summits challenge. He summitted Mount Everest in 1995, Mount Vinson in Antarctica in 1997 and climbed an 8,000m peak (Cho Oyu in Tibet) without oxygen.

CLARE O'LEARY, from Bandon, County Cork, is a Specialist Registrar in Gastroenterology and General Internal Medicine. She has climbed extensively throughout the world. During her travels, she has taken a special interest in children and their education.

She was a member of the successful 2003 Irish Everest Expedition, and returns to Everest in 2004 to fulfil her dream of being the first Irishwoman to stand on the world's highest mountain.

ACKNOWLEDGEMENT: *The Diary of Frederick T. Bear* is an educational project aimed at teaching children about the geography and cultures of the world. The project was initiated by Mary Curtin, teacher in Cloghroe National School, Cloghroe, County Cork.

TO DAIRMUID

FREDDY'S EVEREST DIARY
THE DREAM OF FREDERICK T. BEAR

FOLLOW YOUR DREAMS

PAT FALVEY AND CLARE O'LEARY

Pat. Faly

FREDDY. T. Bear

an lof of all cuml

The Collins Press

Published in 2004 by
The Collins Press,
West Link Park,
Doughcloyne,
Wilton,
Cork

© Pat Falvey and Clare O'Leary 2004

For further contacts and updates of Freddy's travels visit www.patfalvey.com
or freddy@patfalvey.com, tel: 064-44181 or write to Frederick T. Bear
at The Mountain Lodge, Beaufort, Killarney, Co. Kerry

British Library Cataloguing in Publication data.

ISBN : 1-903464-48-x

Printed in Malta

Remainder of the Irish Team

MICHAEL (Mick) MURPHY, deputy leader, is a keen mountaineer, canoeist and sailor and has climbed extensively in many of the great ranges of the world. Michael owns an outdoor pursuits centre in west Cork. He is also a teacher of building construction and outdoor pursuits in St Fachtnas,Skibbereen, County Cork.

GERARD McDONNELL has 6 years climbing experience in Alaska with many expeditions made to the Alaska Range. He likes celebrating summit arrivals by playing a small bodhran that he pulls out of nowhere. Originally from Kilcornan, County Limerick, and now residing and living in Anchorage, Alaska, he works as an automation engineer.

HANNAH SHIELDS has trained and climbed in South America, Scotland and Ireland. She is a top-class athlete, specialising and competing in marathons, triathlons and long-distance running. Hannah lives in Derry, where she now works as a dentist.

GEORGE SHORTEN has trained and climbed in Alaska, South America, Africa,Russia, Ireland and Scotland. He has already succeeded in climbing four of the seven summits (the highest point on each of the seven continents). He works as an anaesthetist at the Cork University Hospital and at University College Cork.

Sherpa Team – Integral part of the Irish team

PEMBA GYALJLI SHERPA-SIRDAR
Sherpa Team Leader

Pemba Gyalji is in charge of our strong Sherpa team on the mountain and shares responsibility with Pat to ensure a successful expedition. The Sherpa team are an important part of the expedition and without their participation we would stand little chance of success. They are all personal friends of Pat's and have worked together on different expeditions over the last thirteen years in Nepal and Tibet. All of the Sherpas are considered full team members and are treated and respected as such.

Between them they have made many notable successful attempts on the world's highest mountains, including Mount Everest

ANG RITA

DAWI

DORJE

MINNGMA CHHIRI

NANG CHEMMI

NIMA

PEMBA RINZEE

The route taken by the 2003 Irish Everest
Expedition and inset, map showing location of
Everest.

www.patfalvey.com

THE IRISH EVEREST EXPEDITION TEAM 2003, FROM LEFT, STANDING:
Pat Falvey, Ger McDonnell, Mick Murphy,
Clare O'Leary and George Shorten;
FRONT, SITTING: Frederick T. Bear and Hannah Shields.

Saturday 15 March 2003

Hi! My name is Frederick T. Bear, though my friends call me Freddy. I'm an adventurer and explorer, and have had many thrilling exploits on my journeys around the world. And now, my most exciting trip yet is about to happen! I am going to climb to the summit of Mount Everest with the Irish Everest Expedition Team. Imagine me, a little bear, on the very top of the world!

There are so many people at Cork Airport to see me off, I feel like a celebrity. Tears come to my eyes as I hug my friends goodbye. But although I am sad to be leaving them for three months, bursts of excitement surge through me. Amid all the cheers of family and friends, our climbing team wave goodbye and head for the plane for the first stage of our trip.

We are on our way!

Freddy

Freddy's schoolfriends saying goodbye.

Freddy on the flight deck, learning to fly.

Sunday 16 March 2003

I gaze out the window of an aeroplane, flying from Abu Dhabi to Kathmandu. This is my fourth flight since leaving Cork Airport yesterday morning. We flew from Cork to Dublin, and then onto Heathrow Airport in London, England. We then boarded a plane bound for Abu Dhabi in the United Arab Emirates. Now finally we are heading for Kathmandu in Nepal, our final destination.

As I get further from home, I started to feel home-sick and a little worried – will it be too cold for me up on the top of the mountain, even with my furry coat ? Will I have a nice warm bed to sleep in, just like home? What about my food? What if this is all a big mistake and this is all too much for a little bear, to climb to the top of the world? 8,848 metres sounds very high up to me! When I look out the window, all I can see are fluffy clouds and blue sky, nothing else. Next time you see an aeroplane in the sky imagine, that is how high Mount Everest is!

I notice Pat Falvey, our team leader and a well-known Irish mountaineer (who summited Mount Everest in 1995) deep in conversation with the man sitting next to him. Pat is explaining to him that you should always follow your dreams. 'If you think you can, you will; if you think you can't, you won't. So, if you set your mind on something, always believe that you can do it.'

What Pat said is true. We have spent months preparing for this trip: getting the proper clothing, equipment and food, training, and learning all about the mountain itself and its secrets. We are ready for anything. I am part of a team, and by working together I know we can succeed.

Just then I felt the plane start to descend and had a popping sensation in my ears. We are approaching the airport at Kathmandu.

Our adventure is about to begin.

Freddy

Sunday 16 March 2003: later that day ...

As we walk through the streets of Kathmandu, I can hardly contain my excitement. Never before have I experienced such wonderful sights, sounds and smells. We are going to spend three days here before we set off to Base Camp and I can hardly wait to begin exploring.

Tomorrow, Pat and the team have work to do. They

have to organise our permits to climb Mount Everest from the Nepalese government.

Freddy

Wednesday 19 March 2003

Yet another aeroplane. This time though, it's a little one, only about twelve people and one little bear on board. We are heading for the small village of Lukla, (altitude 2,800m), in the middle of the Himalayas.

It is a short flight, only about 35 minutes and before I know it, we are approaching Lukla. Once we land, we will rest in a nearby village for a couple of hours and then start on the first stage of the long trek into Base Camp.

We walk for about four hours, heading for a small village called Phakding. Following Pat's example, I sling my backpack over my shoulder and we head off. The rest of our equipment and gear are loaded on the backs of yaks. We lead the way along the rocky, uneven trail, with the Sherpas (Nepalese helpers) following along behind with the yaks. We wander through forests of rhododendrons, alongside rivers and streams, crossing little wooden bridges, and all the time I can see the beautiful Himalayan peaks beck-

Yaks (hairy mountain cows) carrying the team's equipment to Base Camp.

oning me.

My little legs cannot keep up with the grown-ups, so I hop into Pat's bag when he isn't looking. As we hike along the trail, a young Sherpani, whose cheeks are as red as ripe apples, stops us. She is selling sun-tala (mandarin oranges) which I willingly buy from her. They are juicy and very sweet. I notice some wooden huts along the way and we will visit these tea houses tomorrow. I wonder if I can get a hamburger, chips and coke there?

Gotta go set up camp, as we have reached Phakding. I'm starving!

Freddy

Thursday 20 March 2003

Woke at 6.30am. A Sherpa brings a hot cup of tea and a basin of warm water to wash myself in. No bathrooms here! We pack up everything and load them onto the yaks. When we are finished breakfast, we head off again, this time for the village of Namche Bazaar (3,440m).

It is going to take us six hours to get there. As we head off I think I will fall backwards with the weight of my bag. It is heavier than I am! Pat has told us to pack all that we need for the day's hike, so I do. George, another member of our team, notices me struggling and says he had better check my bag. To my dismay, he removes my three jars of honey, my tin of salmon, and my can opener. All that is left in my bag is a warm fleece, a goretex jacket, sunglasses, sunblock, a hat, a camera and my diary. It is much lighter and I head off with a spring in my step.

Halfway through the day's trek, we come to a teahouse. As we enter the gloomy, dimly-lit building, I notice the fire burning merrily in the corner. There is a man placing some sort of fuel on the fire. He tells me it is dried yak dung. My mouth drops open. Yak dung! Yeuch!

The Sherpa cooks, who have come along with us for the trip, prepare our food outside, while we sit inside, at one of the many long tables. While waiting for my food, I go over to the counter to see what type of food you can buy there. They have Pringles, chocolate, popcorn and 7-Up. You can also get local food like yak's cheese, soup, potatoes and eggs. Coffee and tea are also available. The Nepalese drink lots of hot tea, just like the Irish.

Here comes lunch – salmon and honey sandwiches – my favourite!

Freddy

Poor Freddy, in his sleeping bag, suffering from altitude sickness.

Friday 21 March 2003

Ow! Ow! Ow! My head is pounding, my stomach churning, I is one sick bear. Clare, a doctor on our team, explains that I am suffering from altitude sickness. Great! Here I am on one of the most exciting trips of my life and I am stuck in bed in my sleeping bag, miserable.

There is nothing anyone can do for me, my body has to adjust to the high altitude. Clare assures me I will feel better soon. We are camping outside the village of Namche Bazaar at 3440m above sea level. That's three times higher than Carrauntoohill (Corrán Tuathail) (1,041m), the highest mountain in Ireland. In fact, everyone is having a rest day today, to allow their bodies to get used to being up so high in the mountains.

Love to all my friends back home.

Freddy

Saturday 22 March 2003

What a glorious sunrise on Mount Everest, or Chomolungma as the Tibetan people call it. This word means 'Mother Goddess of the Earth'. The sun rises at 6.30am and we all get up early to see it. Tears come to my eyes at its beauty. Excitement and anticipation surge within me at the prospect of climbing it. I remember Pat's words: 'If you think you can, you will. If you think you can't you won't.' Inspired by this I set off for another day's trekking, a very happy bear, ready for adventure.

Next stop, the village of Debouche.

Freddy

Sunday 23 March 2003

Oh, my aching legs. Yesterday, we hiked for six long hours to the village of Debouche (3,820m). On the way there, we stopped at the monastery in Tengboche for a well-earned rest.

This morning we head off on another six-hour hike to the village of Pheriche (4,243m). Unfortunately this afternoon, I have another headache from the high altitude, so I snuggle down in Pat's backpack and go to sleep for a couple of hours. When I awake, everybody is setting up camp. Feeling much better, I hop out to help them.

When we finish, Pat says we should all go to the medical centre in the village to have a check up. The doctors want to be sure our bodies are adjusting well to the high altitude. They will check the oxygen saturation in our blood, our pulse and our blood pressure. I go nervously to the clinic, yet the doctor says I am doing just fine, despite my headaches.

Tomorrow is a rest day, so we will have time to do some exploring. That should be fun, I might even get to ride on a yak again.

Talk to you soon,

Freddy

Monday 24 March 2003

I slept badly last night and woke with a bad headache. My tummy felt really sick too.

This morning I can't eat my breakfast, but Pat makes sure I drink lots of hot, sweet tea. Clare explains that a lot of people feel sick until their bodies get used to the thin air and lack of oxygen. She says it is important to take medicine and not to trek any higher until I feel well again. I go back to bed for the morning and by lunchtime feel a lot better. I get up and have some lunch with the other trekkers and sit by the fire watching it snow outside.

At three o' clock, we go to a lecture on altitude sickness. It is very good and the doctor is very helpful at answering our questions.

Bye,

Freddy

Wednesday 26 March 2003

It was an enjoyable three-hour hike from Lobuche up a rocky trail of moraine from the Khumbu Glacier (moraine is made up of rocks and debris left behind by a glacier).

When we reach the village of Gorak Shep (5140m), we pitch our tents and spend an enjoyable afternoon in the sunshine, getting ready for the climb tomorrow on Kala Patar. Pat says we should go to bed early tonight as we must get up at 2am to start our trek. Great!!! I get to use my head lamp as it will still be dark. Sunrise is around 6.30am and we plan on watching the sun coming up over Mount Everest. I can't wait ...

Freddy

Thursday 27 March 2003

Staggering out of my tent, bleary-eyed, I zip up my warm jacket to protect against the freezing cold wind. 'Let's get going everyone,' says Pat cheerfully, as he heads up the dark trail, guided by the glowing light from his head lamp. I follow him sleepily, missing the cosy warmth of my sleeping bag. It is 4.30am and time to begin the trek up to Kala Patar (5,545m).

Luckily it is an easy climb to the summit and we

Pat and Freddy before their trek through the darkness and inset, Freddy and Clare with trekkers, watching the sun rise over Everest.

are there just in time to watch the sun come up over Mount Everest.

Base Camp at last (5,364m)! Having descended from Kala Patar once again, we trek to our destination. It's time have to say goodbye to all our friends who came to Base Camp with us as they must start to head back to Lukla once again.

As we enter the camp, it looks like a village of tents, with people from all over the world milling around, as they too prepare to climb Mount Everest. There were teams from Japan, South Africa, Canada and the Indian Army team. This year is a very special one as it is 50 years since Mount Everest was first climbed by Sir Edmund Hillary and Sherpa Tenzing Norgay in 1953. Our team plans to follow their route from Base Camp, through the icefall to the Western Cwm and South Col and from there to the summit. So exciting!

When we check to see if our gear has arrived on the yaks, we find some is there, such as our insulation gear, our boots and crampons, ropes and ice-axes. More has still to come – I guess that we can walk much quicker than a yak! Some of our oxygen still hasn't arrived but we have been promised it is on its way from Russia. It is in special light-weight cylinders

The multi-coloured tents of Base Camp.

made of titanium (just like the space shuttle).

We plan on spending two or three days here, planning for the next and most important stage of our trip.
Freddy

P.S. In Base Camp, we have three big tents – one
kitchen tent, for all the cooking, one 'mess' tent, where
we eat and chat, and one storage tent for all the equip-

ment. Each of the climbers has their own tent to sleep in and I am going to share with Pat. There is an Irish flag at each corner of the camp.

Friday 28 March 2003

Today is my first day at Base Camp. I was cold during the night and found it difficult to sleep, listening to the sound of the snow falling outside, and at the same time hearing the creaking and groaning of the ice underneath us. The glacier on which we are camped is constantly moving downhill at the rate of about 35cm a day. In fact, a large crack opened within inches of George's tent from the ice movement during the night. He got a terrible fright when he came out of his tent.

When we got up this morning, we had to take down our tents and set them up again. We had put them up in a big hurry last night as it was freezing cold (-20 degrees Celsius). Not having levelled them properly, I ended up in a bundle at the end of the tent with Pat's elbow in my face!

For the next few days we must relax here at Base Camp so our bodies get used to the thin air and we are ready for the next part of the climb.

Freddy

Monday 31 March 2003

Waking from a very exciting dream, I hear the sound of bells ringing. I slowly crawl to the bottom of the tent and peek out.

Outside about twenty yaks are wandering about, all carrying red and green bags labelled 'Irish Everest Expedition 2003'. Our bags! I pull on my warm clothes and scramble out of the tent to get to the bags as I know there are lots of goodies to eat inside! Usually I am not allowed to eat too many sweets, but up here, it is really easy to lose weight and it's important to eat all kinds of food.

To give you an idea of what we eat at Base Camp here is what we ate yesterday:

Breakfast: rice pudding, warm bread (chapatti) with scrambled eggs and sweet tea.

Lunch: tomato soup, potatoes and vegetables, hot chocolate (and don't tell Pat, but I also scoffed a Bounty bar, when no one was looking!).

Dinner: Vegetable soup, vegetable fried rice, mixed fruit, hot tea. It is also very important to drink plenty of fluids while we are at this height, so I am drinking lots of Lucozade, Tang and hot tea.

Freddy

Wednesday 2 April 2003

Went on an acclimatisation walk today, to help our bodies adjust to the altitude. I am still a bit woozy when I exercise, but am getting better. I don't get very many headaches now either.

Last night, while I was in bed, Pat prepared crampons for my new boots, which I will need to walk in the snow.

These are special attachments which have spikes or points to grasp the snow. I got a bright red pair so that no one will mix theirs up with mine!

We are planning to start the climb on Friday 4 April and I want to make sure I am ready!

When we all got back to camp we had lots of hot noodle soup – yummy. I went to bed for an hour because I was so tired, but got up in time for dinner!

Freddy

Thursday 3 April 2003

I am suddenly jerked awake by a thundering explosion. I stumble out of my tent to see a huge avalanche cascading its way down the valley (an avalanche is a fall of large amounts of snow and ice down a mountain). While we looked on in horror, Pat explained to

Freddy showing off his new crampons.

me that all tents had to be evacuated as an enormous burst of cloud was pushed in front of the main thrust of the avalanche and he was afraid we would be engulfed by this. Luckily, it stopped short of Base Camp. Phew, that was a close one!

More excitement today with the arrival of a shower tent. I rush to be the first to use it and am disappointed to find that, instead of a sophisticated electric shower, there is a bucket, with a tap at its base, hanging off a string, on the roof of a little square tent. And then, to make matters worse, while I am having my shower, one of the others steals my clothes. I have to run around the camp, looking for them, wrapped in a towel, my fur dripping wet. Grrrr!!!

In the afternoon, Pat, Clare, Hannah and I go to see the Khumbu icefall. This is the start of the climb – where we will be tomorrow. The ice is really unsafe to stand on and I have to walk right behind Pat all the time, in case I stand on unstable ice. I am a bit scared about tomorrow, but know that the others will look after me.

Freddy

Friday 4 April 2003

After a restless night, I am first up this morning at 5am. Dressed and ready to go, with my rucksack packed with warm clothes and, of course, plenty of chocolate to keep me going, I bound out of the tent. To my dismay, I see it has snowed heavily overnight.

Pat is talking seriously with Pemba, our Nepalese Sirdar (the person in charge of the Sherpa team) as they stand next to the mess tent. Sensing that something is wrong, I sneak over to find out what is going on. I overhear phrases like 'too dangerous' and 'better wait'. Turning around and going into breakfast, I am disappointed and feel like crying.

Slowly the rest of the team walk in, dressed in their climbing gear. Pat and Pemba follow. Pat explains that the heavy snowfall and high winds during the night could make the icefall too dangerous for climbing so we will have to wait until tomorrow.

I know he is right but can't hide my disappointment. Clare picks me up and says: 'OK, Freddy, back to bed until 9am and then we'll get some more practice with your ice axe, and the ladder crossings.'

Drifting to sleep, my mind is full of what I have been practising: crossing huge crevasses (a deep crack

Clare showing Freddy how to cross the ladder over the crevasse.

in a glacier) using ladders. You have to carefully catch the points of your crampons on the rungs of the ladder and use two side ropes as hand rails. This looks very scary and unstable!

I decide to try my best when practising and to get it perfect for tomorrow.

Freddy

Saturday 5 April 2003

I am first up again today. My rucksack is packed from yesterday and I eat all my breakfast before anyone else!

We are ready to leave at 08.30 hours and I proudly bound along in front of the Irish Everest team. We pass lots of the other camps on our way to the icefall and I feel they are looking at me with respect and admiration (none of them realise how nervous I really am!).

At the foot of the icefall, we put on all our gear (crampons, harnesses and safety carabiners) and start to follow Pemba on the route. I am a little breathless, but don't have time to think about it as I am so busy looking in awe at the huge seracs, ice walls and crevasses (a serac is a huge block of ice).

Before long we come to the first of the ladders; although I had been practising, I got a fright when my

Freddy and the team climbing on ladders over-hanging seracs the height of two-storey houses, with ladders simply tied together.

crampon was too short to fit between the rungs of the ladder. George sees what is wrong and without any fuss scoops me up on his shoulder. I cling on for dear life as we cross unsteadily over the ladder. The crevasse below is so deep I can't even see the bottom; I want to throw something down, but am afraid to make any sudden movements!

I stay put on George's shoulder for the next couple of hours as the team slowly make their way upwards. It is great to get to see such spectacular views without having to do any of the hard work!

We stop for a chocolate break around 11.30 hours. I am starving and take out the Twix bar I had hidden two days previously (when I saw they were running short!). We turn back and make it to Base Camp in time for hot soup and lunch. I am bursting with excitement. I can't wait to get back into the icefall, but I know it is going to be about four days before we are ready to move again.

Freddy

Sunday 6 April 2003

Today was a rest day, which meant a sleep-in until 08.30 hours. I dozed and listened to my walkman while the hot sunshine warmed my tent like a sauna! After breakfast, the team had lots of work to do – organising food supplies. I decided to watch all the

Freddy relaxing with his walkman.

activity. Some of the Sherpas were setting up new tents to be used higher on the mountain whilst some were setting up a place for the puja; this is a special religious blessing for all climbers and Sherpas. It is given by one of the Buddhist lamas (priest or monk) from a monastery in Pangboche. Nepalese people

Freddy sitting amongst items to be blessed at the puja.

believe this blessing keeps them safe on the mountain, and they do not climb without it.

Freddy

Monday 7 April 2003

Being first up this morning, I head off for a quick walk before breakfast, dressed in my warmest jacket because it was freezing outside. As I amble along, I suddenly hear a loud grumbling noise, which gets louder and louder, followed by a tremendous crashing sound. I dash behind a boulder. Peeping out from behind it, I watch in horror as I see a huge cloud of snow heading towards Base Camp. A great big avalanche! I'm beginning to regret coming out on my own. 'Oh, no', I think, and hope Pat and the others will wake up before it is too late ...

As I watch in terror, I hear footsteps behind me and see Pat with his camera pointed towards the mountain. 'Hey, Freddy,' he shouts, excitedly. 'It's OK, we're safe here. This is really big avalanche. So keep following it!'

Feeling safer with Pat standing close, I stare as the cloud of snow grows and gathers speed, tearing down the mountain. It's like something from a horror film, but seems to gradually dissolve as it comes closer to Base Camp. Wow, what a start to the day! Relieved that we have escaped danger once again, I head off with Pat to the mess tent for breakfast and to tell the others what they've just missed.

I spend the afternoon giving the Sherpas a hand to organise things for the puja.

Freddy

Tuesday 8 April 2003

There is a buzz of activity all about the camp when I wake this morning, and I have barely enough time to finish breakfast before it is time to head to the puja! Clare and Hannah put me sitting next to some burning juniper for the ceremony. I'm afraid my fur will catch fire, so they move me to the very front of the altar, where I can oversee everything.

Each of the climbers has brought a piece of their climbing equipment to be blessed (I brought my ice axe.) As I sit among the items to be blessed, I notice the dough animals we had made and even bottles of coke.

Sitting opposite the lama and his helpers, I watch as they chant and pray. Then the blessings begin and everyone throws rice and flour in the air! Following this, bottles of blessed 'Mount Everest whiskey' are passed around. Yeuch!

Once the chanting is finished, the Sherpas begin to raise prayer flags from the altar to the four corners of Base Camp. In the middle of all of these are the Irish and Nepalese flags. What a sight!!

Then comes my favourite part: the singing and dancing! All the Sherpas join hands and dance togeth-er – and our team try to learn the steps too! Next come the Irish songs: the *Fields of Athenry, Molly Malone* and so on. The party continues for a couple of hours and then people slowly start to leave. I am exhausted and head back to my tent for a quick nap. I can't wait to get started now that we have all the blessings.

Freddy

Wednesday 9 April 2003

It is time to sort out our supplies for the next couple of days on the mountain. We need to make sure we have plenty of food and are bringing special energy drinks called scandishakes in addition to our regular meals. If we don't eat enough, we will lose weight and not be strong enough for the long days of climbing ahead. I love picking out my favourite bars and drinks!

Tomorrow we plan to head to Camp One, (19,500ft, 5,943m). This will take us through the icefall and on to the plateau beyond.

Guess what Nima Sherpa told me today? Last year, two dogs made it to Camp One! Their team mates carried them across the ladders and they walked the rest of the way themselves. I was really impressed. Now I don't feel so bad about having to get a lift across the ladders too!

I have to go and pack my rucksack for tomorrow before it gets too late – we must bring our sleeping bags, warm clothes, head torches, and of course, our crampons and ice axes. I hope I don't forget anything!

Fingers crossed that the weather will be good for us.

Freddy

Thursday 10 April 2003

We have an early start this morning – up at 7am and ready to head for the icefall at 8.30am. As I leave the Camp, I am surprised by the weight of my rucksack – it feels like someone has piled rocks into it during the night! I plod along behind the team, puffing and pant-

Freddy with some of his
climbing gear.

ing. I'm glad when we reach the bottom of the icefall and have to stop to put on our crampons and harnesses and get out our ice axes. I grab a quick drink of Lucozade and am ready to start again. It is a long, slow haul. I keep making excuses to stop – to put on my sun cream, to have a drink, to take off my rucksack. None of the climbers seem to be struggling but between the weight and the heat of the sun, I am having great difficulty keeping up.

At around midday, we stop as by now, everyone seems to be getting tired. We have been on the move for over three hours and are less than halfway to Camp One. I don't think I can keep going, but feel I can't tell the others how exhausted I feel. Just as we are about to head off again, Pat says 'OK, jump on Freddy' and he kneels down for me to jump on top of his rucksack. I am so relieved; I think I am going to cry. I am sore all over, with blisters on my heels from walking in my big boots and I feel so tired. As I settle on top of his rucksack, I have a brilliant view of the icefall. I hold on tight as we cross the ladders and even tighter as we climb the ice walls.

I think I must have fallen asleep for a little while because when I wake, it has got colder and we are just starting to see the tents at Camp One. We are moving slowly but steadily and there are already a few teams there ahead of us. Soon after we arrive, we get into our tents, sleeping bags and down clothing. We tuck into some hot soup and pasta and head to bed really early. I fall asleep as soon as my head hits the pillow.

Freddy

Saturday 12 April 2003

We all sleep in late this morning as we have planned an easy day. After a late breakfast we get geared up again. Our plan is to head towards Camp Two, just to see the route and get a bit of exercise. Everywhere looks completely different – like a football field made of snow and ice! Everything seems easier without the weight of our bags, and the scenery is amazing.

At one point on our climb down, the fixed line we are attached to for safety (to avoid falling into a crevasse) disappears behind some big ice blocks which had fallen the previous day. Ger has just passed through and is being followed by George, who is in the centre of this ice field. Suddenly an explosive sound, like a bomb exploding, can be heard. Mick roars 'Run George', and above his shout, everyone hears a crashing sound. We turn to see a huge block of ice crack off and hurtle in George's direction. He runs furiously in the opposite direction, narrowly escaping it as it crashes to a halt just behind him. Apart from having got a fright though, George is fine. We all decide to move a little more quickly to get out of there as soon as possible. The icefall is living up to its expectations.

We get back to Base Camp at lunch time and tuck into more hot soup and lemonade. I crash for the afternoon, but am delighted with what we have done in the past couple of days, glad to know that we can have a break at least until after the weekend.

Freddy

Sunday 13 April 2003

Having spent most of the morning in Base Camp sorting our high altitude food packs and supplements for Camps Two to Four, I notice Pemba Rinji, one of the climbing Sherpas, come into the mess tent at tea time, limping painfully.

Having left Base Camp at 4.30am, he crossed the icefall and climbed up to Camp Two. He was taking up some of our supplies. On the way back down, he twisted his ankle badly. It was very swollen and he was in a lot of pain. Clare gave him some ice packs to put on it and I helped him to hold them – they felt really cold. Then she put some cream on it and a special support bandage. He felt much better then and had a cup of tea with us, which really cheered him up.

Freddy

Monday 14 April 2003

We have to organise our supplies for Camps Two and Four into loads of 13kgs. The Sherpas are not allowed carry packs any heavier than this when climbing up beyond Base Camp. That still sounds heavy to me! In the high altitude, everything is more difficult and climbing alone is a struggle.

Can you imagine, it takes you about two minutes to climb four metres up here?

Freddy

Friday 18 April 2003

Having been stuck here for days, I'm really sleepy this morning when we are called for breakfast. It is only 4am and I lie in bed after Pat calls me, secretly hoping that he will come back and say the weather is still too bad! No such luck. We are on the move in no time and

Freddy hanging out at his tent.

it makes a big difference moving without bags on our backs, and before the sun has come up. Hannah explains the reason why we have to get up so early is that we don't want to get caught in the icefall in the midday sun as it is too dangerous. The ice starts to move as the day gets warmer and large blocks of ice come tumbling down. I wouldn't like to get hit by one of those!

We do some great climbing today as a team, on fixed ropes and ladders, going up, down and every which way. We make it to Camp One in about four and a half hours, and last time it took us almost seven hours.

I am very proud of myself when we finally arrive. I jump into the tent and curiously watch as Mick and Hannah start to melt snow so they will have water to drink and cook.

Freddy

Saturday 19 April 2003

The walk from Camp One to Camp Two is shorter, but because the team have to carry all their gear, it means I have to carry my own rucksack and I find myself puffing behind the others! I am a little worried also as Pat has mentioned we will be walking through the 'Oven' today. I follow the others towards the Western Cwm (a cwm, also called a coom, a cirque or corrie, is a basin with steep sides and gently sloping floor, in mountainous regions, caused by the erosive action of ice).

Although we can see the tents at Camp Two in the distance, the journey is all uphill (for two or three hours) and seems never-ending. Looking around me, I can see that we are surrounded by mountains. Mick points out the different mountains to me: Mount Everest, Nuptse and Lhotse. Mick tells me that Lhotse is 8,501 metres high and is the fourth highest mountain in the world. As we go along, I notice it getting hotter, as the sun's heat is trapped around us. It is so warm we have to stop every five minutes for a rest, as we feel we are baking on ice! Now I know why Pat called it the 'Oven'!

During the afternoon at camp, I heard Pat talking to Pemba about bad weather. The wind was howling outside the tent, and I could feel the tent base lifting under me like a magic carpet!

The winds continued to thrash the tent and suddenly there was a deafening crash. Two big, empty tents behind ours had been knocked by the winds. Pat said he was going outside to secure our tent with Mick and not to worry!

Freddy

Sunday 20 April 2003

After breakfast, Hannah and Clare bring me to their tent. They give me a palm-pilot with games on it.

Hannah explains these are special tests to see how the brain is working high on the mountain, where there is less oxygen than at home. The tests are analysed by NASA scientists, who believe the effects may be similar to those on astronauts when they are in space. I have to match shapes, colours and so on. It definitely seems harder than it should. The others had to radio Base Camp to do more tests.

We relax for the afternoon. We need to rest more during the day up here and get breathless even while speaking; not exactly a walk in the park!

Freddy

Monday 21 April 2003

This morning as I lie in bed, I hear lots of noise outside. I know I won't get back to sleep, so wander out to see what is going on. Pemba says there has been an accident in the icefall and that two of our team's Sherpas (Mingma and Nang Chemmi) are heading down to help with the rescue. I beg him to allow me to come with him, and see what's going on. He is reluctant and says it would be too dangerous, but then gives in and says I can come if I stay on his shoulder and man the radio. It feels like a real adventure!

We reach the scene of the accident in less than 45 minutes. A huge chunk of ice, the size of a house, had collapsed as two Sherpas crossed what had been a small crevasse, with the aid of a ladder. One Sherpa had already been rescued and seemed to be OK. The second lay groaning in agony in the crevasse.

Pemba tells me to radio Base Camp immediately and get them to contact the medical clinic to arrange a helicopter rescue. I feel really important as I pass on this message. Everyone moves quickly then, as a group of Sherpas carefully haul the badly injured man up out of the crevasse. They carry him to Base Camp where the helicopter arrives within minutes to take him to Kathmandu.

We then head back to Camp Two. The weather is still stormy with snow and gusting winds so we can't do any climbing. The storm is supposed to be over by tomorrow evening and then we can get a little higher on the mountain, maybe even to Camp Three, before we head back down to Base Camp for a rest.

I have a dry cough and a slight headache. Clare says not to worry, as it is the result of the dry air and the high altitude. There is only 50 per cent of oxygen in the air compared to air at sea level. So everything

Freddy radioing Base Camp to send for help.

we do is three times harder. This is one tough mountain to climb!

Freddy

Tuesday 22 April 2003

I wake with a headache this morning, and lie in bed feeling tired and groggy. I can't eat my breakfast, but drink plenty of hot, sweet tea that Hannah and Clare make for me. My cough has kept me awake during the night. I lie back in the mess tent and begin to fall asleep. When I wake, half an hour later, Pat's saying it would be a good idea to go for a walk, to get some exercise. My headache is improving, so I grab a fist of jelly beans and get ready to leave. Ger laughs, saying I couldn't be that sick if I could still eat jelly beans! I insist I am, and grab another fistful for the trek!

We set off uphill; it is pleasant at first, but then begins to snow heavily and we start to get very wet. Pat says it would be better to turn back. I agree with him wholeheartedly! I eat a huge dinner and then win three games of cards. Yippee!

Freddy

Wednesday 23 April 2003

We are up at 4am again and I carefully get dressed in my warmest clothes, woolly hat and mitts. The Sherpas have made breakfast, but I feel sick when I look at the eggs and toast set in front of me. The team push me to eat it and say I will need the energy.

When we are all finished breakfast, Pat warns us to make sure our fingers and toes are nice and warm before we leave camp. We will not be able to reheat them in the severe conditions higher up on the mountain and we could get frostbite.

We head out into the cold morning, aiming to make it part-way to Camp Three. I am shivering violently, my fingers are numb with the cold and I generally feel miserable. I try to walk a little faster, thinking that will warm me up, but I get so caught for breath I have to stop for a rest. Nobody is speaking as we plod slowly along. I feel really sorry for myself and want to go home, but am afraid to turn back on my own.

After about an hour and a half, we reach the Lhotse face. This is like a steep wall of hard ice that we have to climb using our jumars (a jumar is a clamp with a handle that can move freely up the rope it is clipped onto but locks when downward pressure is applied).

We point the front-points of our crampons into the hard blue ice to give us a secure grip.

I reluctantly make my way upwards, my fingers numb with the cold and I can no longer feel my toes. I begin to cry, hoping no one will notice. George grabs my hand. 'Freddy,' he calls, 'put these mitts on and we'll head back.' I'm so relieved, I cry more loudly. We turn and begin to abseil down. As we reach the bottom of the face the sun begins to come up and I finally begin to feel a little warmer. Still shivering, and with my teeth chattering uncontrollably, I look back at what we have just climbed and feel really proud. As the others catch up with me, they each slap me on the back and shout, 'Well done, Freddy, we're on our way!' We are all in great form by the time we reach Camp Two and celebrate with a hearty breakfast (two breakfasts in one day!) before collapsing into our tents to rest.

Freddy

Thursday 24 April 2003

I am first out of bed this morning, anxious to head back to Base Camp to tell everyone my news. Mick offers to give me a piggy back. We head down the glacier together, through the 'Oven', as quickly as we can, before the sun gets too high in the sky, remembering how hot we had felt the last time we were there.

As we pass Camp One, we pick up some belongings we had left behind. We soon reach the scene of the accident in the icefall and I proudly explain to the others what had happened. We decide to keep moving quickly through this dangerous spot. Within a few hours we are back down to Base Camp; Dawi and Kami come out to greet us and have made my favourite lunch – fried egg and chips, with loads of tomato ketchup!

After lunch we queue for hot showers and a much-needed change of clothes. We rest again for the afternoon, delighted to be back to familiar (and safer) territory.

Freddy

Friday 25 April 2003

It is really warm in the tent by 8am and I have to go outside to cool off. It's funny, Base Camp is much warmer now than when we first arrived. Climbers wander around in shorts, t-shirts and hats during the day!

Since all the teams have to take turns going up the mountain a timetable is organised. It could get really crowded at the top if everybody was there together, since there are more than twenty teams at Base Camp. After all, the top of the world is only the size of a snooker table! We are going to be one of the first teams to summit (12-15 May). I'm delighted when I hear this.

Freddy

Sunday 27 April 2003

Pat calls a team meeting today to discuss what we are going to do next. Here is our action plan: we will head back up to Camp Two on Tuesday, 29 April/Wednesday 30 April. From here we will continue up to Camp Three and stay at that camp overnight. Next morning we will try for Camp Four. I hope we make it and that it won't be as cold as last time!

I can't believe my ears then when Pat announces we will come down the mountain, past Base Camp, to the village of Debouche, 3820 metres, where we will spend seven days relaxing and building up our strength again. When the week is over, it's back up the mountain again, even higher this time! We are like yo-yos going up and down the mountain!! But we are getting closer to the top each time. I can't wait to stand on the top of the world.

Talk to you next week.
Freddy

Tuesday 29 April 2003

Up at 3am this morning and have a warm, hearty breakfast before setting out from Base Camp for the icefall. Even though we have crossed the Khumbu ice-fall many times now, we have to take care each time as it is one of the most dangerous glaciers in the world.

It's around 5am when we start on the route and we make good progress. Luckily, it isn't too cold. We continue without a break for about three and a half hours.

On reaching Camp One, we stop for ten minutes and have a drink and some chocolate. I am amazed when Pat says, 'OK gang, let's go. Break is over'. It's tough starting out again, but we have to keep going. It snows as we travel through the Western Cwm. It's as if somebody has turned the 'Oven' down!

Exhausted after nearly seven and a half hours of climbing, I fall in the door of the mess tent at Camp Two and drink a big mug of juice. Soon Cadge, one of the Sherpas, brings in warm noodle soup. That is my limit though and I fall asleep alongside my empty bowl.

Freddy

Wednesday 30 April 2003

When I wake this morning, I feel much better. It snows heavily all day, which means we are stuck in our tents. I go out, planning to build a snowman but suddenly sink into deep snow up to my neck! Once Ger rescues me, I thank my lucky stars, as I am whisked away to get some clean, dry clothes on – building a snowman isn't that important anyway!

There was a huge serac fall in the icefall this morning. Seracs as large as houses crashed off each other, creating a domino effect. Some climbers were trapped and terrified, as they did not know which direction the blocks of ice were coming from. Luckily, nobody was hurt. I am glad that I wasn't there when it happened!

Freddy

Thursday 1 May 2003

The sky is clear when we check at 5am so we head off to the foot of the Lhotse face. It is a tough seven to eight hours on the mountain today, much harder than usual. The difficulty is caused by having to wade through soft snow; every time I take two steps forward, it feels like I am taking one back! I am really struggling, and also afraid that I will get lost in the deep snow, especially

Freddy up to his neck in the snow.

dreading the climb up that 1,200-metre wall of ice. What a challenging climb that is! Boy, this is one tough adventure for a little bear.

Freddy

Friday 2 May 2003

I don't feel hungry or thirsty this morning, but the others make me drink three hot cups of tea. We left Camp Three around 11am. I am glad to be leaving there; something about it makes me feel scared and sickly.

I catch up with George and head down with him. We abseil down the steep face – whee! It was great fun. What had taken us hours to climb up yesterday, only took 90 minutes to get down today. I can't wait to abseil again – it is really cool! George lets me go down some of the ropes on my own (using my figure of eight) and carries me on the steeper sections. He's moving slowly and tells me he feels really tired. We catch up with the others at the bottom of the Lhotse face and walk towards Camp Two together.

Freddy

Saturday 3 May 2003

We get up early this morning and pack up. I'm relieved

Freddy using a device to climb up
the ice wall (jumar).

we are heading back to Base Camp – it almost seems like home now after over seven weeks.

I jump up on my usual spot on Pat's rucksack and take off pretty quickly. Soon Hannah, Clare, Ger and Mick go out of sight. I notice George is falling behind so I hop out of Pat's rucksack and wait for him. I ask him if he's OK but he doesn't answer me, just sways unsteadily on his feet. I call out to Pat. George complains that he has double vision and feels faint. We decide to get him back to Base Camp as quickly as possible as the situation is serious.

Guided carefully by Pat, and fainting three times, George somehow manages to make it down through the icefall. I wish I could help George, but know the most important thing is for him to get down. I radio base for help and at the bottom of the icefall Dawi and Kami are waiting anxiously for us with warm juice for George. We head straight for the medical clinic, which is just a big blue tent.

Within minutes the doctors start to treat George with special injections. They say that he has High Altitude Oedema (swelling of the brain) and will have to be airlifted by helicopter to the hospital in Kathmandu tomorrow. They place him in a Gamow

George being helped down by the Sherpas to the helicopter.

bag (a decompression chamber) for a while, which looks like an inflated sleeping bag that you are completely zipped into and has a little window you can see out. This will make him feel much better. Although he is really weak, he keeps trying to chat to us. During the day, we all stay with George, as we are worried about our friend. Mick says he will stay up with him all night at the clinic to make sure he is OK. Giving him a big hug as he lies on his bed, I walk sadly over to my tent … Poor George.

Freddy

Sunday 4 May 2003

Holding on tightly to Hannah's hand so I won't get blown away, I watch the helicopter land outside Base Camp. I start to cry as George heads over to it; it is hard seeing him so unwell and I know we will all miss him a lot.

Seeing me standing there, forlorn and with a tear-stained face, Pat picks me up and heads over to the mess tent. He tells me we should be very proud of George and all he has achieved. Climbing Mount Everest, he explains, is not just about reaching the top – it is about the journey, about meeting people, about team play and doing one's best. He says that George is a perfect example of all those things and we are honoured that he was a member of our team.

Freddy

PS. Pat just got a phone call from George in the hospital to say that he was feeling a lot better.

Monday 5 May 2003

We get up around 7am this morning and pack our rucksacks. This time we are heading down the valley for a rest and to try to eat lots as we have all lost weight. Everyone's face is really sunburned from being on the mountain; I am glad that I have fur!!!! Their lips are badly chapped and mine are very sore as well. Pat said they will be much better in a few days.

The team take off at top speed from Base Camp and don't stop until they arrive in Lobuche, where we eat non-stop for two hours!

We continue down to a village called Debouche and are staying in a gorgeous little teahouse there called Ama Dablam Garden Lodge. Beautiful rhododendron forests surround the village and I cannot wait to explore. There is also a great view of Ama Dablam mountain, known as the Matterhorn of the Himalayas, which is 6,814 metres high.

We will be taking it easy here for another few days before heading back to Base Camp. I can't believe we will be heading for the summit the next time we head up the mountain!

Freddy

Tuesday 6 Friday 9 May 2003

Pat has a sore back. He says it is a trapped nerve. I'm not sure what it means but it seems very painful. He is afraid he might not be able to climb if it does not get better. I give him a hug to cheer him up.

Freddy

Saturday 10 May 2003

Our stay in Debouche has done us good; we ate like kings, our chapped lips are better, sunburn is gone and we are feeling great. The big push to the top of Mount Everest is on. Yippee ...

When leaving, we hear a noisy bunch of Irish accents arriving through the main door! They are doing the Everest Base Camp trek and are driving overland from Melbourne to Dublin to raise funds and awareness for cystic fibrosis (CF).

Among the goodies this Irish party brought along were a hurley and sliotar and Ger is going to try and do a *puc fada* from the summit of Everest! I hope he

Freddy and Mick relaxing.

won't be the cause of any unexpected injuries!

After they leave, we head for Pheriche. It is much easier walking this time, now that our bodies are used to the lack of oxygen in the air.

Everyone is getting really excited about the climb

*Ger, Hannah and Freddy
with the hurley and sliotar.*

now, but worried about the bad weather. I hope everything works out OK .

Freddy

Sunday 11 May 2003

We are staying in another really nice lodge here in Lobuche and are just two to three hours now from Base Camp. People are fed up, waiting for the weather to improve, but it's just too dangerous to climb until the winds settle.

Yesterday two Sherpas returned from the mountain with severe frostbite on their fingers from the intense cold. This is scary – they may end up losing some of their fingers. I hope everything will be OK for our team.

Freddy

Sunday 12 May 2003

We are up early again this morning to start our final trek towards Base Camp. We have a four to five hour walk ahead, but nobody minds; we are heading back for the final time.

On our way, we see a huge Malaysian flag, which a group of Malaysians have placed close to the route to Kala Patar.

Kala Patar is 5,545 metres high. It is a great viewing point for Everest, the Khumbu glacier and the Changri glacier. There is also a great view of Pumori

Base Camp from there. Pumori Mountain is right behind our Base camp and is 7,165 metres high.

Everything is still in order at Base Camp and Tenzing, one of the cooks, makes us a pizza as a special treat. It feels good to be back at base. Nobody knows when we will be moving up the mountain because the weather is really unreliable. Hopefully it will be soon.

Freddy

Friday 16 May 2003

At 3am, Dawis shakes my tent, waking me with a start. It is time to get going! I jump out of bed, wanting to be ready first! I do my best to eat all my breakfast so I'll have plenty of energy on the climb! We reach the icefall by 4.30am and start out together as a team. I'm with Mick, because Pat's back is still sore. We get through the icefall in about four and a half hours. At that stage, we become separated and I can no longer see Pat, Hannah or Ger, but Clare is just in front of me. As we carry on, I can see she's getting slower and keeps stopping to rest. I whisper to Mick that something must be wrong, but he tells me to leave her for a while. After another while, we stop and

Clare abseiling.

sit down for a short rest. Mick chats with Clare and tries to cheer her up because she's feeling really miserable. She has picked up a stomach bug. Nima Sherpa offers her a cup of hot tea. Heading off again, she seems to get slower and weaker. Mick is really good and stays with her the whole time; after a while Pemba, one of our Sherpas, arrives down the glacier with hot juice for Clare, and then takes her rucksack to carry it for her. We all set off once more (Pemba is really kind).

It is lunch time when we arrive at Camp Two. Clare is even weaker now, having got sick a number of times. She lies on the floor looking pale and wretched. Everyone is very concerned. If you get sick above 20,000 feet, your body can't recover.

Freddy

Saturday 17 May 2003

Exhausted from our climb yesterday, we all sleep in until around 8am this morning. Although it is a rest day, it gets so hot in the tent I can't bear to be in there any longer. I go to see if Clare is any better. She gets up for breakfast, but doesn't eat or drink much. Pat decides to spend an extra day at Camp Two to give her a chance to improve. It seems as if the whole of Base Camp is up here or on the way up at the moment. We meet the Indians, French, Belgian, Americans and lots more.

Freddy

Sunday 18 May 2003

We have lots of work today – organising food, medicine and oxygen. We all put on our oxygen masks and regulators, as we need to make sure everything is working and fitted properly. The mask feels strange on my face when I try it on, and when I walk around; I can't even see my feet! Pat says we all have to go outside for a while, wearing all our gear, to try and get used to it. It's really cool. During the afternoon, everyone wants to call home to speak to their families before they for the summit and into a place called Death Zone.

Freddy

Monday 19 May 2003

We get up at 3.20am. Everyone is quiet, deep in thought, knowing this will be our final few days on the mountain. Even though Clare is still sick she will give it a final try and hope she will get better. When

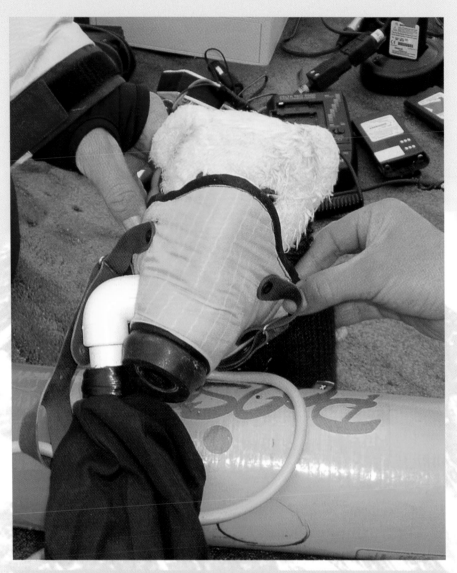

Freddy trying out his oxygen mask.

we are nearly ready to leave, Pat looks at me and says, 'Freddy, I think you'd better hop into my rucksack for the first couple of hours until the sun comes up'. The climb from Camp Two to Camp Three is long and difficult. As we move on, I can hear the crunching of crampons on the ice and snow in every direction around me.

After some time Pat speaks to Clare and he sounds very serious. I hear words like 'sick', 'Base Camp', and 'safety'. Clare is feeling very ill and has made the decision to return to base camp to recover for her own safety and the safety of the team.

Although she has been to Camp Three (at 24,000 feet) before, without oxygen, a stomach bug has depleted her of all her energy due to dehydrationand as she moves up the mountain, sickness is making her weaker. I feel so sorry for her. After 65 hard days walking, climbing, crawling and struggling on the mountain and only two days from the summit, she now has no choice but to turn back. Dorje Sherpa will return with her.

I know she is really upset. As Pat gives her a hug, I bury my face in his jacket s I don't have to watch. She is crying and so are Pat and Dorje as they day farewell. I look up with tears in my eyes just in time to give her the thumbs up before we turn away.

We set off again up the Lhotse face and there are crowds of people all around us. As we move slowly along, I manage to pick out Mick, Ger and Hannah among all the climbers but it is sad not seeing Clare anywhere.

We arrive at Camp Three at around noon. I jump onto Pat's sleeping bag as the others gather into the tent. The tent is deathly quiet, everyone upset that another team member is gone. I am going to miss Clare so much, and she will be terribly disappointed to have had to give up, when she was so close to the top, but she and Pat made the right choice; it was too dangerous for her to continue as she was still very unwell.

After a time, we begin to melt snow for drinking water and cook some food. When we finish dinner, we settle down to sleep, wearing our oxygen masks.

Freddy

Tuesday 20 May 2003

We wake around 7.30am when we get a radio call from Base Camp. Clare has made it safely down and

Mick, Freddy and Hannah preparing specialised strengthening food in the tent.

is feeling a little better.

Today we will be heading for Camp Four. On our way there, we will again use oxygen and wear our masks and goggles. We will rest for a few hours there and then we hope to head for the summit late tonight (9-10pm) making it there tomorrow morning. Until I get back down to Base Camp, I won't be able to send you any photographs or updates, but will do so as soon as I can. Keep your fingers crossed and say a prayer that we will all be safe.

Freddy

Wednesday 21 May 2003

Onwards to the summit! I wake at 7.30am, freezing in my sleeping bag. Clare and the others at Base Camp have been in contact, wanting to know whether we had made it to the top or not the previous day. We had all been so exhausted after trying really hard that nobody had radioed them to tell them that sadly we had not made the summit. I could hear Pat explain what had happened. Secretly I hoped we would be heading down, as I was very tired, and a little scared but Pat sounded keen to give it another try.

We try to eat some breakfast. There is silence as we eat and drink though, as everyone thinks about what lies ahead of us.

After breakfast I can hear Pat talking seriously to

Pemba. All around us many teams are packing up and heading back down the mountain. Some of them didn't have enough oxygen to survive another night; others are just too wrecked to stay at this height any longer. There is an eeriness as the Camp empties and again I feel fear. Although it has been my dream to make it to the summit of Mount Everest for many months now, I had no idea how tough it would be and how dangerous it would feel. I am glad to have Pat,

Hannah and Freddy climbing a steep slope.

Ger, Mick and Hannah there with me all the time. I really miss Clare and George.

Later in the day, Base Camp call us again with the forecast. Although high winds are expected, Pat and Pemba decide we will go for it as the forecast has been unreliable and the night looks good. We have Clare and George's oxygen which will be enough to survive another night.

Feeling fear and excitement, I have to have a rest before we begin climbing again, but can't sleep. I'm coughing a lot from the dry air and this wakes me each time I begin to doze off. Eventually, I fall into an uneasy sleep tossing and turning as I struggle through the snow in my dreams.

Within hours, we are on our way again, and once more, I find myself perched back up on Hannah's pack. The winds are quieter this time, unlike the fearsome gales last night, and I don't feel as afraid. We walk slowly together as a team and keep a check on each other's oxygen. Running out of oxygen up there could make any of us sick.

As we climb, I keep looking at Hannah's watch; I pray the sun will come up so that our hands and feet will warm up as it is freezing cold and I don't want to get frostbite.

Oh, I really hope we make it this time ...

Freddy

Thursday 22 May 2003

By 5am, I am so cold I start to cry. I do all I can think of to warm up. I look around at the other climbers, trying to keep an eye on Mick, Ger and Pat. Suddenly, Hannah stops. She turns to Nang Chemmi (the Sherpa with us) and Pat, and says, 'I can no longer feel my fingers or toes. I'm afraid I'm getting frostbite and will have to turn back.' Pat offers to tuck me into his down suit to keep me warm but I feel I have to stay with Hannah. 'No,' I say to Pat, 'I have to go back with Hannah. Helping my friend is more important than getting to the top.' I am repeating something Pat has often said. Hannah is looking really sad at the idea that she has to stop climbing, but then she smiles at me and says, 'Thanks Freddy, I really appreciate what you want to do, but I will be fine as I will have Nang Chemmi with me. Try to get to the top for me, as you are still OK'.

Crying I jump off her pack, and give her a big hug and kiss before Pat snuggles me in under his down

Pat and Freddy watch from the South summit as team members climb within an hour of the summit of Everest.

suit. I look on sadly as Hannah turns and begins to make her way downwards.

I stick with Pat for another six hours of climbing,

listening to his panting and the slow beat of his footsteps. We seem to be getting slower and slower. This alarms me, because I have always regarded Pat as the strongest. I can see the South Summit ahead. I get a fright when Pat glances down at me; he looks completely exhausted. When I check his oxygen gauge I find it isn't working. I start to fiddle with it, twisting and turning it to see if I can fix the problem, and eventually a gush of oxygen makes its way to his mask. Pat looks relieved. He has had very little oxygen for many hours now and I tell him he looks drunk. I can see he's worried as we are now in a very dangerous situation.

On arriving at the South Summit, and just one hour from the top of the world, Pat decides it would be dangerous for him to continue to the summit as he is exhausted from the lack of oxygen. He is my climbing partner now so I will have to stick with him. For a while I'm disappointed as we are nearly there. Pat explains how his friends have died on Everest though, because of bad decisions, and that to continue would only put our lives at risk.

The rest of our team are just ahead and Pat tries to radio them to let them know of our decision to stop. We can see them but the radios don't work and we cannot make contact.

He then tells me not to be frightened. He says that we cannot go ahead but we should wait for Mick, Pemba Gyalje, Ger and Pemba Rinje to make sure everyone gets down safely together.

He explains that because his bottle of oxygen hasn't worked he is hypoxic (which means that he hasn't got enough oxygen in his body) and because of this his eyesight is blurred and he is not physically able to continue. He might fall, or collapse, and have to be rescued Not only would this put him in danger but it could put the rest of the team in danger also. So we sit it out on the South Summit, and watch proudly as the rest of our team continue to the top of the world.

For three hours we wait in the icy cold at -35 degrees Celsius (it's only -7 degrees Celsius in your freezer!). Pat explains to me that when you climb a huge mountain like Everest, you cannot always guarantee reaching the summit and that it is best to be safe and not take any foolish risks. He says that when any member of the team summits, we succeed as well, because we are part of the team. Each one of the team is responsible for the success of the expedition. I tell him I don't mind that I won't make it to the tip top, but that it is really cool Ger, Mick, Pemba Gyalje and Pemba Rinje are going to do it. I am very proud of all that we have done as a team.

Eventually, after two to three hours, we see Mick, Ger and both Pembas in the distance, heading our way. Their faces are glowing with excitement and I know they have been to the summit. I am delighted for them and call out congratulations as best I can through my oxygen mask.

Ger comes over, stares at Pat intently, and immediately turns his oxygen up full. 'Pat, are you OK?' Pat answers a mumbled 'Yeah. Just watch me as we go down. My eyesight is blurred and I cannot make out the footsteps ahead'. We slowly move down the mountain, helped by Pemba Gyalje and Ger. Later, Pat tells me that he owes his safe return to Ger and Pemba.

It takes a long, slow, five hours before Camp Four comes into sight. To my relief, Hannah comes out to meet us and together they help Pat into the tent and feed him warm fluids. He begins to look brighter within a few minutes.

Mick arrives at Camp Four before us, and when he sees us he starts jumping around and hugging everybody, with an enormous grin on his face. We radio

Base Camp to let them know we are all safe and well and they sing us a muffled version of *For he's a jolly good fellow*. Before long, we are all snuggled up in our sleeping bags, ready for a well-deserved sleep.

Freddy

Friday 23 May 2003

We are up at 6am to eat the last of our food and begin to pack our gear at Camp Four. I look on in admiration as the Sherpas begin to take down the tents and pack huge rucksacks to carry down to Camp Two. They are such kind, loyal, hard-working friends. We leave Camp Four at 8am and began the slow descent to Camp Two. We are all really tired and moving slowly. By the time we reach Camp Three, everyone is running out of oxygen. It is almost 5pm before we eventually reach Camp Two.

Although tired, we are all dying to call home and tell everyone the great news. I fall asleep on the floor of the mess tent while the others are still on the phone!

Freddy

Saturday 24 May 2003

I wake with a mixed feeling of excitement and relief.

It is hard to believe these would be our final few hours on Mount Everest, after almost eleven weeks of hard work! As I lie there, I think about home, school, my friends, the team I had been with while climbing here, and the Sherpa team who have been so good to us. What an experience – I think I must be the luckiest bear in the world! Hearing me shuffling around in my sleeping bag, Pat wakes up. 'Does it bother you that you didn't make it to the summit?' I tell him that although I would have loved to get there, I actually feel really happy with what I have achieved. I was part of a great team who looked after me and cared for me for the past three months, four of our team members made it to the summit and I know I did my very best to get as far as I did. It would have been dangerous to go any further, and seeing Pat sick had given me a fright; I knew I couldn't have left him on his own without getting help. I had helped each of my friends in their moment of need, first George, then Clare and Hannah, and finally Pat; their health and safety were much more important than reaching the summit of Mount Everest. Pat was proud of me, and once we'd had a hug, we went for breakfast before the final descent to Base Camp, and some celebrating!

Mick, Freddy and trekker Ann Kelleher celebrating at Base Camp, where the team's names were posted on the inside of the tent.

Clare has come up the icefall to meet us and the others greet us below with flags and coca cola! When we get to our Camp, we see a big 'congratulations' sign, with all our names posted on the inside of the tent. I feel a huge sense of pride to be part of this group. Back in the now familiar mess tent, we party and tell stories late into the night.

Freddy

Sunday 25 May 2003

We spend most of today tidying and packing our gear, ready to be taken down the mountain by yaks. It seems strange to be emptying the tents that had been our home for so many weeks, but the thought of finally being able to sleep in a real bed is nice.

At about 2am, we finally turn in, only to have to struggle out of our sleeping bags at 5.30am the following morning! We have decided to get a helicopter out of Base Camp.

A happy and proud Freddy on the plane home with some trekkers.

We have a brilliant flight – I can't sit still, there is so much to see. I look around non-stop. We land safely in Lukla and from there catch a flight back to Kathmandu.

I'm feeling really tired after this expedition I am going to take a break here for the next few days. I can't wait to get home now and and see all my friends. I hope you enjoyed hearing all about my travels. Goodbye for now!

Freddy

Some of the team with Manus O'Callaghan and the Lord Mayor of Cork, John Kelleher, on their triumphant return to Cork.

Epilogue
Sunday 3 August 2003

When I got home from Everest, I had a really busy few weeks meeting up with friends, meeting the President at the Áras, celebrating and building back my strength (eating lots of good food!).

Rebecca, Ian and Mary Curtin, Freddy and President of Ireland, Mary McAleese and Clare in Áras an Uachtaráin.

As the hype was beginning to die down and I was trying to get back to normality, I began to wonder 'what next?' One evening, as it came close to my bedtime, I got a call from Pat. We chatted for a while, then his voice changed and in a serious tone he said, 'Freddy, I want you to have a think about going back to Everest next year. Clare and John Joyce (Base Camp manager) both want to return and have asked if I will lead the expedition again. I've agreed and would love for you to come back too. I will need to start organising and training in the next few weeks.'

I remained silent on the other end of the phone. Although it had been a tough trip, my heart leapt with excitement at the thought of getting another opportunity to climb Mt Everest. I told Pat I would call him by the end of the week.

I went to bed, but couldn't sleep. I tossed and turned thinking about what lay ahead. I knew there was only one answer for me ... I was going to go back; and the thought of being able to go back with Pat as leader and as part of an Irish team made me certain. I was back on to Pat the following morning. 'Count me in,' I said, hardly able to control the excitement in my voice. 'I'm delighted, Freddy, I know you can do it', was Pat's reply.

I was delighted when Pat called me a week later to see if I wanted to do some training on Howling Ridge on Carrauntoohil (Corrán Tuathail). This is one of the mountaineering routes on Ireland's highest mountain in Kerry. We arranged to meet at 8.30am Monday.

I carefully packed all my gear the night before – helmet, harness, rope, boots and climbing rack. I counted down the hours as I lay in bed, restless with excitement. As we drove towards Kerry, Clare and I chatted about going back to Everest as she is really keen to return too. Both of us know there will be a lot of training again this year, but she loves that. And so do I! She told me John Joyce is going to climb with us next year – I really liked him and he is a great singer!

As we arrived at Lisleibane, I could see Pat's jeep ahead. We were the first of the climbers to arrive and the sun was already shining brightly. It was a spectacular morning to be out on the hills.

I was dying to get started. When Pat told me I could lead the route, I gleamed with joy. I felt a little nervous, but had been up a couple of times before which helped. I was trying to be really careful, which slowed us down, but nobody seemed to mind.

By 1pm, we had most of the tricky bits done and ate our sandwiches. We could see the lakes far below and I felt really proud as I looked down where we had climbed. After lunch, we gathered everything together and packed it back in our rucksacks before walking to the cross at the summit of Corrán Tuathail.

As the weather was so good, we decided to continue on and scramble over the Binn Cearach ridge to the summit of Binn Cearach and from there to Knockbrinnea and back down to Lisleibane.

What a day! Eight hours of brilliant climbing in one of my most favourite parts of the world.

I have lots of plans for training before my return to Everest; these include the French Alps for a week, Mount Cook in New Zealand, Aconcagua in South America and a week in Scotland. What a life!

Pat is delighted with the progress I am making and has even asked me to join him on a really amazing journey to the South Pole in 2005/2006 as part of the three poles expedition. I can hardly wait!

Join me on all these exciting adventures by following the Freddy links on www.patfalvey.com

See you soon,

Freddy

Freddy's Passport

Name: Frederick T. Bear
Born: 25 December 1968 in the
North Pole
Age: 7 bear years (1 bear year = 5
human years)
Home: The Mountain Lodge,
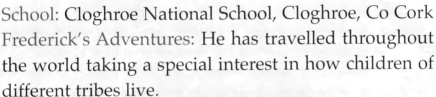
Beaufort, Killarney, County Kerry
School: Cloghroe National School, Cloghroe, Co Cork
Frederick's Adventures: He has travelled throughout
the world taking a special interest in how children of
different tribes live.
Dream: To climb Mount Everest, the world's highest
mountain.
Training: Freddy began climbing in County Kerry,
Ireland. He has spent much of his time doing moun-
taineering courses in Ireland, Scotland and the Alps
learning the skills required to be a good mountaineer.
These include rope work, navigation, camp craft, glacier travel, first aid and rescue techniques.

His adventures so far have taken him to far away
places, including Europe, America, Russia, Africa,
Peru, Argentina, Chile, Nepal. He has climbed some
of the most beautiful mountains in the world.

Also available from
The Collins Press

Ice Man – The Remarkable Adventures of Antactic Explorer Tom Crean: Michael Smith

ISBN: 1-903464-44-7 Price: €7.99

The frozen land of Antarctica is not for ordinary people but Tom Crean was no ordinary man. When he was fifteen he ran away from home and joined the navy. His next step into the unknown took him to the Antarctic wilderness where he spent even more time than the famous explorers Scott or Shackleton. He explored the unknown, crossed ice fields and wild oceans, and courageously saved his friends from death.

The Boss – The Remarkable Adventures of Ernest Shackleton, Heroic Antarctic Explorer: Michael Smith

ISBN: 1-903464-57-9 Price: €8.99

When he was sixteen, Irishman Ernest Shackleton left school to join the merchant navy and went on to become one of history's greatest explorers and legendary figures. His extraordinary adventures of endurance and survival in the Antarctic have thrilled generations. Here, for the first time, an established authority on the history of Polar exploration has written about Shackleton's gripping exploits especially for children.